SUPERNATURAL SCIENCE

GHOST
INVESTIGATORS

BY
MADELINE TYLER

Gareth Stevens
PUBLISHING

Please visit our website, www.garethstevens.com. For a free color catalog of all our high-quality books, call toll free 1-800-542-2595 or fax 1-877-542-2596.

Cataloging-in-Publication Data

Names: Tyler, Madeline.
Title: Ghost investigators / Madeline Tyler.
Description: New York : Gareth Stevens Publishing, 2020. | Series: Supernatural science | Includes glossary and index.
Identifiers: ISBN 9781538253038 (pbk.) | ISBN 9781538253045 (library bound) | ISBN 9781538254127 (6 pk)
Subjects: LCSH: Ghosts–Juvenile literature.
Classification: LCC BF1461.T95 2020 | DDC 133.1–dc23

First Edition

Published in 2020 by
Gareth Stevens Publishing
111 East 14th Street, Suite 349
New York, NY 10003

Copyright © 2019 Booklife Publishing
This edition is published by arrangement with Booklife Publishing

Written by: Madeline Tyler
Edited by: John Wood
Designed by: Drue Rintoul

All images are courtesy of Shutterstock.com, unless otherwise specified. With thanks to Getty Images, Thinkstock Photo and iStockphoto. Front Cover – Fer Gregory. 2 – Joe Techapanupreeda. 4&5 – andreiuc88, goa novi, Angela Schmidt. 6&7 – andreiuc88. 8&9 – Michal Ludwiczak, Syda Productions. 10&11 – Cody DeLong, pockygallery, Tom Tom. 12&13 – Pla2na. 14&15 – Alex Kolokythas Photography, stuar, Hayati Kayhan, Third of november, Inked Pixels, Tomas Ragina. 16&17 – Baimieng, Pati Photo, Kittibowornphatnon, DR-images, Poy Panurat, PlusONE. 18&19 – Siyapath, mainfu, The7Dew, kasha_malasha, plampy, Joe Therasakdhi. 20&21 – drasa, Africa Studio, Hurst Photo, Miyuki Satake. 22&23 – Zoe Sopena, atdr, Chinnapong, Jason Salmon, travelview, Hollygraphic. 24&25 – Pavel_Markevych, drasa. 26&27 – Tatiana Popova, struvictory, Chris Sagherian. 28&29 – Netfalls Remy Musser, witoon214, Marco Barone. 30 – Anki Hoglund.

All rights reserved. No part of this book may be reproduced in any form without permission in writing from the publisher, except by a reviewer.

Printed in the United States of America

CPSIA compliance information: Batch #CW20GS: For further information contact Gareth Stevens, New York, New York at 1-800-542-2595.

CONTENTS

PAGE 4   What Are Ghosts, Anyway?
PAGE 6   Language of a Ghost Investigator
PAGE 8   It's Time to Investigate!
PAGE 10   Predictions and Results
PAGE 12   Investigation 1: Cold Spots
PAGE 16   Case Study: Hampton Court Palace
PAGE 18   Investigation 2: Sounds and Interference
PAGE 22   Case Study: Salem
PAGE 24   Investigation 3: Spirit Photography
PAGE 28   Case Study: Catacombs of Paris
PAGE 30   Debrief
PAGE 31   Glossary
PAGE 32   Index

WORDS THAT LOOK LIKE THIS ARE EXPLAINED IN THE GLOSSARY ON PAGE 31.

What Are Ghosts, Anyway?

Do you ever feel like there's someone right behind you, breathing down your neck or tapping you on the shoulder? Maybe it feels like you're always being watched, but when you turn around to look behind you there's no one to be seen.

Don't worry – you're not the only one who feels like this. If you've picked up this book and seen the title, then you may already have guessed that the cause of all this paranormal activity might be... ghosts.

HAUNTS, APPARITIONS, PHANTOMS, SPOOKS... DID YOU KNOW THAT THESE ARE ALL DIFFERENT NAMES FOR THE SAME THING?

Ghosts are said to be the spirits that remain on Earth after a person has died. They usually have some unfinished business that they need to attend to before they can rest in peace. Most are believed to be friendly and don't cause any trouble. They might move things around in your house, or accidentally make your TV go a bit fuzzy from time to time, but don't worry – they'll leave you alone if you leave them alone! Some people believe that ghosts exist, and other people might not. It's a ghost investigator's job to get to the bottom of the mystery.

If you want to become a real ghost investigator, then you'll need to learn the science behind the spooks. Where do cold spots come from? What's making things go bump in the night? And what are those weird spots that keep appearing in photos? Fear not, young investigator. Soon, all will be revealed, and you'll be a top ghost hunter in no time.

However, this is not a mission for the **FAINTHEARTED**. Some ghosts can apparently be very dangerous, and they definitely shouldn't be messed with. Evil spirits have reportedly taken over houses, graveyards, hotels, and even schools. They can slam doors, shatter glass, and make your life a living nightmare. So, if this all sounds like too much, close this book now and no one will ever know. But if you're feeling brave enough, turn the page and begin your supernatural journey...

A PLACE IS SAID TO BE HAUNTED IF A GHOST DWELLS THERE.

Language of a Ghost Investigator

If you want people to believe that you're a real ghost hunter carrying out real scientific investigations, then you'll need to learn the right words to use. Scientists often use lots of long, complicated words that might not seem to make much sense. Don't worry – these words are just fancy ways of talking about something quite simple.

ACCURATE:
careful and free from mistakes

ANALYZE:
to examine something carefully in order to explain and understand

AVERAGE:
the typical amount or most central number of a range of numbers

CONTROL VARIABLES:
the parts of an experiment that are kept the same

DEPENDENT VARIABLES:
the parts of an experiment that you measure

ESTIMATE:
to make a careful guess about something

EVIDENCE:
something that gives proof and can be used to give reason to believe in something

FAIR:
playing by the rules, or treating everything and everyone equally

INDEPENDENT VARIABLES:
the parts of an experiment that you change

MEAN:
the number you get when you add a list of numbers up and divide it by how many numbers there are in the list, giving you the average number

MEDIAN:
the number in the middle of a list of numbers when the numbers are ordered from lowest to highest or from highest to lowest

MODE:
the number that appears the most often when a list of numbers is ordered from lowest to highest or highest to lowest

PLOT:
to mark data points on a graph

PRECISE:
exact, specific, and accurate

PREDICTIONS:
guesses of what will happen in the future

RANGE:
the difference between the biggest and smallest number. You can find the range by taking the smallest number away from the biggest number

RELIABLE:
can be trusted

FLICK BACK TO THESE PAGES IF YOU COME ACROSS A TRICKY WORD WHILE READING THIS BOOK.

It's Time to Investigate!

Working Scientifically

Before you head out into the big, wide world in search of ghosts and ghouls, it's important that you know exactly how to carry out a real scientific investigation. It can be very hard to keep your cool and stay calm when there could be a ghost waiting for you around every corner. However, if you want people to take your research seriously, you'll need to make sure that you carry out all of your investigations like a true scientist, no matter how scared you might be. Remember, seeing a ghost is one thing, but getting other people to believe you is another challenge altogether. Have you got your thinking cap on? You'll need some carefully planned investigations, the right equipment, and a whole load of questions that need answers.

Science is all about getting the most accurate information. Here are some questions to ask yourself during your investigation:

- Am I using the right equipment?
- How can I make sure that my investigation is fair?
- How can I make my measurements more accurate and precise?
- Will changing different things in my investigation affect my results?

You may think that being brave is the most important part of your mission as a ghost investigator, but that's only part of it.

The first step of any investigation is to **IDENTIFY** what it is that you're trying to find out. Are you trying to find the temperatures of cold spots in your house, or are you studying sound recordings for any signs of ghostly **INTERFERENCE**? This will help you to decide what equipment you need and how you will need to use it. It's very important to use the right equipment carefully to make your measurements accurate and precise. This will help to make sure that your results are as reliable as possible. Reliable results will mean that your investigation can be trusted.

Predictions and Results

One of the first things you need to do when starting an investigation is make a prediction about what you think will happen. Predictions are important because they make us think about the investigation and what we think the results will be. We have to consider what it is that we're trying to find out and what we think will affect the results.

When you make a prediction, you have to think about how changing different variables might change what happens in your investigation. Would looking for ghosts during the day be harder than during the night? What might happen if you search in different rooms of your house? Do you think there's anything that might make ORBS more likely to appear?

I predict...

Whatever your prediction is, you should always write it down in a notepad. This will keep your investigation focused and give you something to think about when you carry out the test.

As you carry out your investigation, you need to make notes of your results and findings. Try to ask yourself questions as you go through your results, as this will help you to analyze them. Did you notice higher levels of paranormal activity than normal? Why do you think that was? What would you change about your experiment for next time?

Sometimes, it's easier to understand your results if you plot them on a graph. Whether it's a pie chart, a bar chart, or a line graph, all graphs are useful. They also make your investigation look a lot more scientific! People will believe that you really know your stuff.

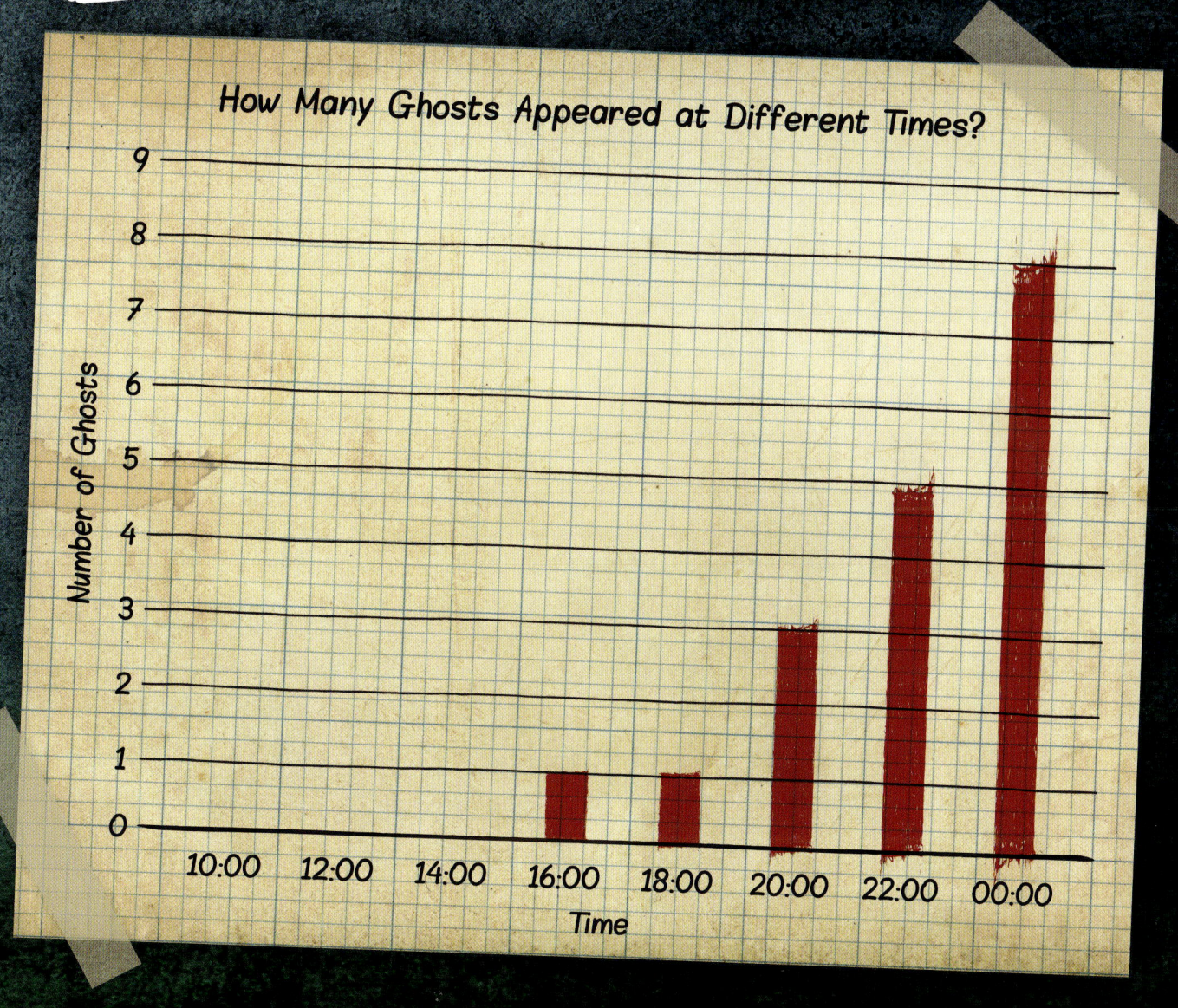

How Many Ghosts Appeared at Different Times?

(Bar chart showing Number of Ghosts vs Time. Y-axis: 0 to 9. X-axis: 10:00 to 00:00. Bars at 16:00 ≈ 1, 18:00 ≈ 1, 20:00 ≈ 3, 22:00 ≈ 5, 00:00 ≈ 8.)

Remember, any ghost you find will not care much for science. They won't care about research, results, or your fancy graphs. They won't hang around to make sure that you've collected enough data before disappearing into the shadows, and some may even try to **SABOTAGE** your investigation. If your results do look a bit funny, it might be a good idea to repeat your investigation a few times.

Investigation 1: Cold Spots

If you're worried that your house might be haunted, don't panic. Ghosts are usually invisible, but they're easy to spot once you know what to look out for. Whether it's a glowing orb in a photograph, or strange bumps in the night, ghosts leave plenty of hints and clues that they're around. However, most ghosts don't want to be found, so many of these signs that ghosts leave behind are there by accident.

Any top ghost hunter will tell you that cold spots or chilly breezes are a sure sign that there's something spooky nearby. Of course, it could just be an open window, but do you really want to risk it? Cold spots are areas of very cold air that may have dropped in temperature very suddenly and for seemingly no reason. Walking through cold spots often gives people a sudden chill that seems to reach right down to their bones. There are no rules when it comes to cold spots. They can appear anywhere and at any time, so you always need to be ready for them.

So, you now know what cold spots are. But why are they there? And how do they get there? Some people say that ghosts are made up of energy and, in order to exist, they must continually take energy from their **SURROUNDINGS**. Energy can't be created from nothing, so ghosts would have to use energy that already exists and **CONVERT** it to something new. Energy can come in many forms, including heat energy. Ghosts may pull heat from the surrounding air and use it to give them strength and power. This makes the air around them suddenly much colder, creating cold spots.

Cold air sinks. This is because cold air is **DENSER** than the warm air around it. However, cold spots act slightly differently. They can rise or sink depending on where the ghost is and how it's moving around.

Where Are the Most Cold Spots?

Do some rooms in your house seem more haunted than others? Some people notice that there are high levels of paranormal activity in their bedrooms, but almost nothing at all in rooms such as the kitchen. If this is the case for you, you'll need to carry out a scientific experiment to compare these two areas.

You will need:
- Flashlight
- Notepad
- Pencil
- Thermometer

REMEMBER TO MAKE PREDICTIONS OF WHAT YOU THINK WILL HAPPEN IN YOUR EXPERIMENT.

Method:

1. Ghosts usually come out in the dark, so turn off all the lights and grab your flashlight.

2. Head to the room that you think might be haunted and grab your thermometer. Try to be as quiet as possible – you don't want to scare any of the ghosts or make them jump!

3. Wander around the room for 10 minutes and record in your notebook the temperatures that appear on your thermometer.

4. Repeat the experiment in the room that isn't haunted and compare your findings. Which room is colder? Did you find any cold spots? Where were they?

Remember to keep track of all your variables:
Independent variable (the thing you change): the room in your house
Dependent variable (the thing you measure): temperature
Control variables (the things you keep the same): time of day, whether the windows are open or closed, and whether the heat is on or off

BE CAREFUL OUT THERE, GHOST INVESTIGATOR. IT'S ALWAYS A GOOD IDEA TO BRING A VIDEO CAMERA WITH YOU TO RECORD YOUR INVESTIGATIONS. IF SOMETHING STRANGE HAPPENS, YOU'LL NEED EVIDENCE!

When you've finished your experiments, it's important to compare your two sets of results. Where did you find more cold spots? Which room do you think had more ghosts in it? Were you surprised by your results? Are they similar to your predictions or are they very different? Remember, you can always repeat your experiment if you think it will make the test fairer. If you do, you can analyze your results for each room and find out what the mode, median, mean, and range are.

Case Study: Hampton Court Palace

If you're keen to find some ghosts out in the wild, then you'll need to know some common hot spots that are popular with ghost hunters.

The building of Hampton Court Palace in Greater London in the UK was started by Cardinal Thomas Wolsey in 1515. Wolsey was one of King Henry VIII's most trusted **ADVISERS**, but eventually Wolsey and the King fell out and Henry VIII took Hampton Court Palace for himself. By 1530, Hampton Court Palace was one of Henry VIII's favorite palaces. At the time, it was very modern and had plenty of space to **HOST** and entertain important guests from around the world. Henry VIII loved Hampton Court Palace so much that he brought all six of his wives there. His third wife, Jane Seymour, died at Hampton Court and his fifth wife, Catherine Howard, was arrested there and later had her head chopped off at the Tower of London.

King Henry VIII

Jane Seymour

Catherine Howard

Since both Jane Seymour and Catherine Howard met their tragic ends at Hampton Court Palace, there have been reports of strange noises, unexplained cold spots, and even sightings of ghostly figures walking through the palace.

The Silverstick Stairs

Henry VIII spent his whole life hoping and praying for a son, so when Jane Seymour, his third wife, gave birth to Edward in October 1537, she became his favorite wife so far. When Jane died just days after this, Henry VIII was heartbroken. According to some reports, a pale figure often appears on the Silverstick Stairs, the very same stairs that once led to the room that Jane died in, on the anniversary of Jane's death.

The Haunted Gallery

Henry VIII wasn't heartbroken when Catherine Howard died. In fact, he ordered her death and wasn't even around to say goodbye to her when she was dragged off by the guards! It's reported that Catherine broke free from the guards and ran along what is now called the Haunted Gallery, screaming out for **MERCY** from the king. Catherine never reached the king, and it's said that her screaming ghost repeats this journey and will do so forevermore...

Investigation 2: Sounds and Interference

Knocking

Many people first report their house as haunted when they hear a knock, knock, knock from inside the walls or behind a cupboard. Whether they're knocking on walls, windows, or the front door, a knocking sound usually means that the ghosts in your house are bored and are trying to get your attention. These ghosts are said to be mostly harmless, and there's usually no reason to worry.

Footsteps

If there are ghosts in your house, it's likely that they have been there for a long time. They may have even arrived long before you showed up. By now, these spirits probably feel very at home walking up and down your corridors at night. If you listen carefully, you might just be able to hear the footsteps as they pass by your bedroom door…

Voices

If you start hearing voices in the middle of the night, you might think it's just a dream. Sometimes it might be, but what if it's not? Some ghosts are said to laugh and sigh, and others can produce bloodcurdling screams that almost sound human. It's easy to mistake these voices for a real living, breathing person. If they're strong enough, some ghosts can reportedly say whole words or even sentences.

Electronic Voice Phenomena

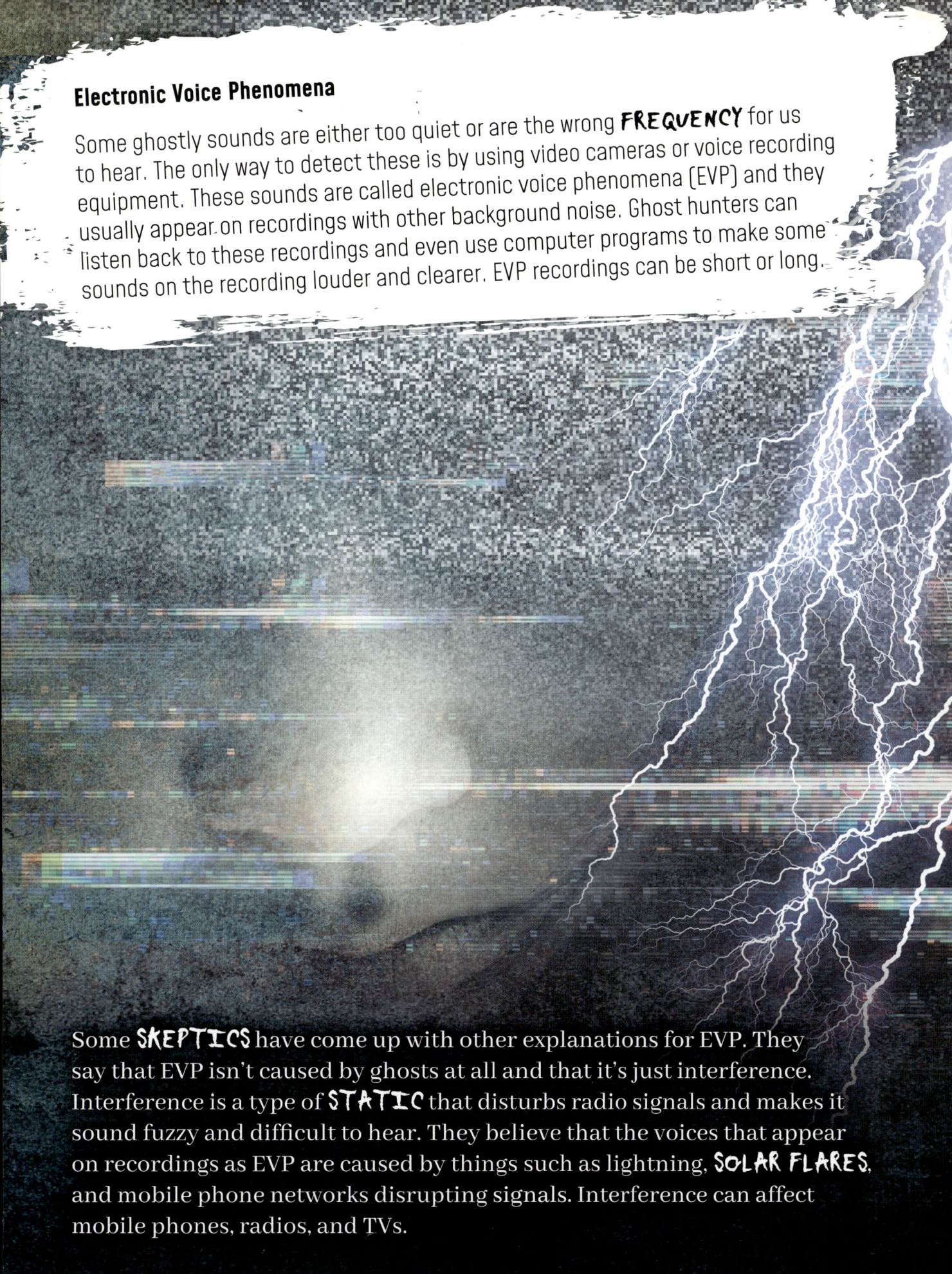

Some ghostly sounds are either too quiet or are the wrong **FREQUENCY** for us to hear. The only way to detect these is by using video cameras or voice recording equipment. These sounds are called electronic voice phenomena (EVP) and they usually appear on recordings with other background noise. Ghost hunters can listen back to these recordings and even use computer programs to make some sounds on the recording louder and clearer. EVP recordings can be short or long.

Some **SKEPTICS** have come up with other explanations for EVP. They say that EVP isn't caused by ghosts at all and that it's just interference. Interference is a type of **STATIC** that disturbs radio signals and makes it sound fuzzy and difficult to hear. They believe that the voices that appear on recordings as EVP are caused by things such as lightning, **SOLAR FLARES**, and mobile phone networks disrupting signals. Interference can affect mobile phones, radios, and TVs.

Are Ghosts Noisiest During the Night?

The strange voices coming from your radio and the fuzzy picture on your TV could be caused by interference, but you can never be too sure. According to some of the best ghost hunters out there, ghosts feel most comfortable and are most VOCAL at night. You'll need to carry out a scientific investigation to see if there's a popular time for EVP in your house.

You will need:
- Flashlight
- Notepad
- Pencil
- Video camera or voice recorder
- Clock or stopwatch

WHAT DO YOU PREDICT WILL HAPPEN?

Method:

1. Wait until the middle of the night, turn off all the lights, and grab your flashlight.

2. Head into the haunted room of your house and set up your recording equipment.

3. Make a note of the exact time you start recording and stay there for 10 minutes.

4. Repeat your experiment during the day and listen back to your recordings.

5. Listen for EVP or interference. Record how long each occurrence of EVP lasts. Is it just a few seconds, or does it last for a few minutes?

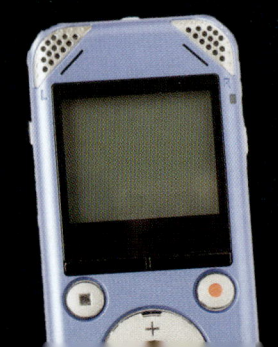

Remember to keep track of all your variables:
Independent variable (the thing you change): the time of day (day or night)
Dependent variable (the thing you measure): sound
Control variables (the things you keep the same): the room in your house

CAN YOU PICK OUT ANY WORDS FROM YOUR RECORDINGS?

What did you find out from your experiment? Do you think the ghosts were more active at night, or did you pick up more EVP during the day? Maybe there were similar amounts of EVP during the day as there were at night. Sometimes, an experiment has to be repeated many times before the results are clear and reliable. You may need to repeat your investigation every day and every night for a whole week before your results are clear. When you're all done, you can plot your results on a graph. It can sometimes be useful to find the mean from a set of results. Finding the mean for this experiment will tell you what the average length of your EVP recordings is.

Case Study: Salem

Between the early 14th century and the late 18th century, witch hunts were a huge part of European **SOCIETY**. During this time, people were very religious and **SUPERSTITIOUS**. They believed that witchcraft was real and that it was the work of the devil.

The Salem witch trials took place in the Massachusetts Bay **COLONY** in America between 1692 and 1693. During this time, many people in the UK and the US were Puritans. The Puritans were English Christians who didn't agree with how the Church of England was run. They didn't like how some parts of the Church of England were still quite similar to the Catholic Church. They were very **SUSPICIOUS** of anyone who didn't follow the very strict religious rules and rules of society within the colony. The trials began in January 1692, and many of the people that were targeted and accused of witchcraft were **SLAVES**, **QUAKERS**, and outspoken women.

> AT THE TIME, BEING A PURITAN WAS ILLEGAL IN ENGLAND. MANY PURITANS MOVED TO AMERICA, WHERE THEY SET UP COLONIES AND COULD FOLLOW THEIR RELIGION WITHOUT BREAKING THE LAW.

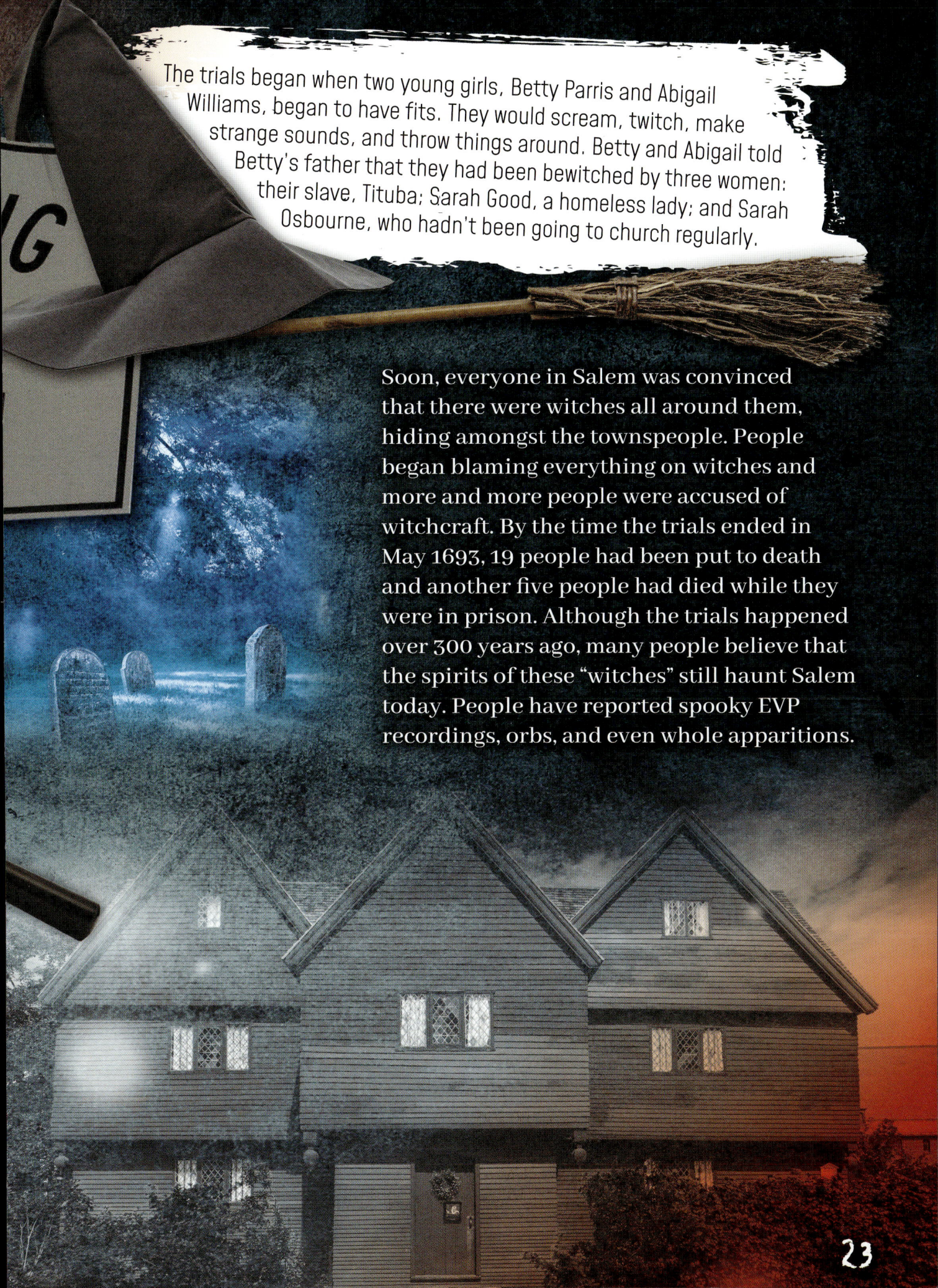

The trials began when two young girls, Betty Parris and Abigail Williams, began to have fits. They would scream, twitch, make strange sounds, and throw things around. Betty and Abigail told Betty's father that they had been bewitched by three women: their slave, Tituba; Sarah Good, a homeless lady; and Sarah Osbourne, who hadn't been going to church regularly.

Soon, everyone in Salem was convinced that there were witches all around them, hiding amongst the townspeople. People began blaming everything on witches and more and more people were accused of witchcraft. By the time the trials ended in May 1693, 19 people had been put to death and another five people had died while they were in prison. Although the trials happened over 300 years ago, many people believe that the spirits of these "witches" still haunt Salem today. People have reported spooky EVP recordings, orbs, and even whole apparitions.

Investigation 3: Spirit Photography

Ever since very early photography, people have been trying to capture ghosts on camera. However, it's not as simple as pointing the camera and clicking away. Ghosts are very camera shy, so it's extremely rare to capture a clear photograph of an apparition or ghostly figure.

Early photographers knew how difficult it was to photograph ghosts, so many of them created fake photographs. They did this by using two or more images to create one photograph. This is called multiple exposure, and the photographers were called spirit photographers. Lots of people were tricked by these photographs and paid lots of money to have their photograph taken with the ghosts of dead family members. One famous spirit photographer was William H. Mumler. He made lots of money from these photographs before he was accused of **FRAUD**.

Orbs

Nowadays, people don't use multiple exposure to create spirit photographs. Instead, many people report ghosts in their photographs in the form of orbs. Orbs are said to be paranormal beings that have taken the simple form of small, glowing circles. Orbs are unusual because they are invisible to the **NAKED EYE** and can only be seen through a camera after a photo has been taken. They come in many different colors, shapes, and sizes. Just like people, no two orbs are the same. Some are clear, some are cloudy, some are purple, and some are green. Many paranormal investigators believe that these colors all mean different things and can tell you if a spirit is trying to **COMMUNICATE** with you.

Some orbs look like human faces. Sometimes these faces look angry or scared, and sometimes they don't have any expression at all. In some photographs, it can be hard to make out if something is a face or not.

Are Orbs Caused by Dust or Spirits?

Some people think that orbs are just the result of digital flash photography. They believe that the camera's flash reflects light off insects, dust, pollen, or even raindrops. Whether you believe this or not, it's always a good idea to carry out a scientific investigation. This way, you can gather evidence to help prove that what you believe is right.

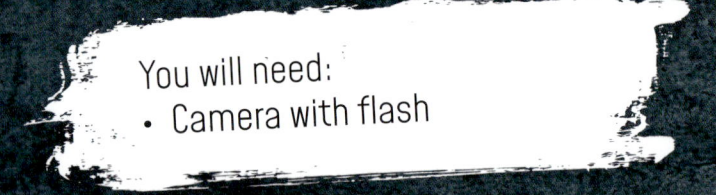

You will need:
- Camera with flash

WHAT ARE YOUR PREDICTIONS? DO YOU THINK THE ORBS WILL ONLY APPEAR IN A ROOM FILLED WITH DUST, OR ARE ORBS REALLY SPIRITS THAT CAN APPEAR ANYWHERE AND AT ANY TIME?

Method:

1. Wait until the haunted room has become dusty. Close the door and don't let anyone clean for at least a week.

2. Wait until nighttime, then grab your camera and head inside.

3. Kick up some dust and take a photograph with the flash on.

4. Now clean the room and open the windows.

5. The next night, repeat your investigation.

6. Take a photograph in the clean, haunted room with the flash on.

Remember to keep track of all your variables:
Independent variable (the thing you change): amount of dust
Dependent variable (the thing you measure): how many orbs are in each photo
Control variables (the things you keep the same): the room in your house

EVEN WHEN YOU DON'T BELIEVE IN SOMEONE'S EXPLANATION, YOU CAN STILL INVESTIGATE THEIR IDEA IN A SCIENTIFIC EXPERIMENT.

Did your investigation teach you anything new about ghosts and orbs? Did orbs appear in all of your photographs, or were there more when it was dusty? Have a look over all of your photos and see how your results compare with your predictions.

REMEMBER: BEING WRONG ISN'T ALWAYS A BAD THING. IT GIVES YOU A CHANCE TO LEARN NEW THINGS ABOUT THE WAYS THAT OTHER PEOPLE THINK.

Case Study: Catacombs of Paris

There is a **NETWORK** of tunnels 65 feet (20 m) below Paris that stretches for over 186 miles (300 km). The tunnels are home to the Catacombs of Paris, which hold the remains of around 6 million people. The tunnels were first built in the 13th century but weren't used to bury people until the 18th century. By this point, Paris had grown so much that its graveyards were running out of space to bury everyone. People began to empty the cemeteries in 1786. It took 12 years before all of the bones were moved underground.

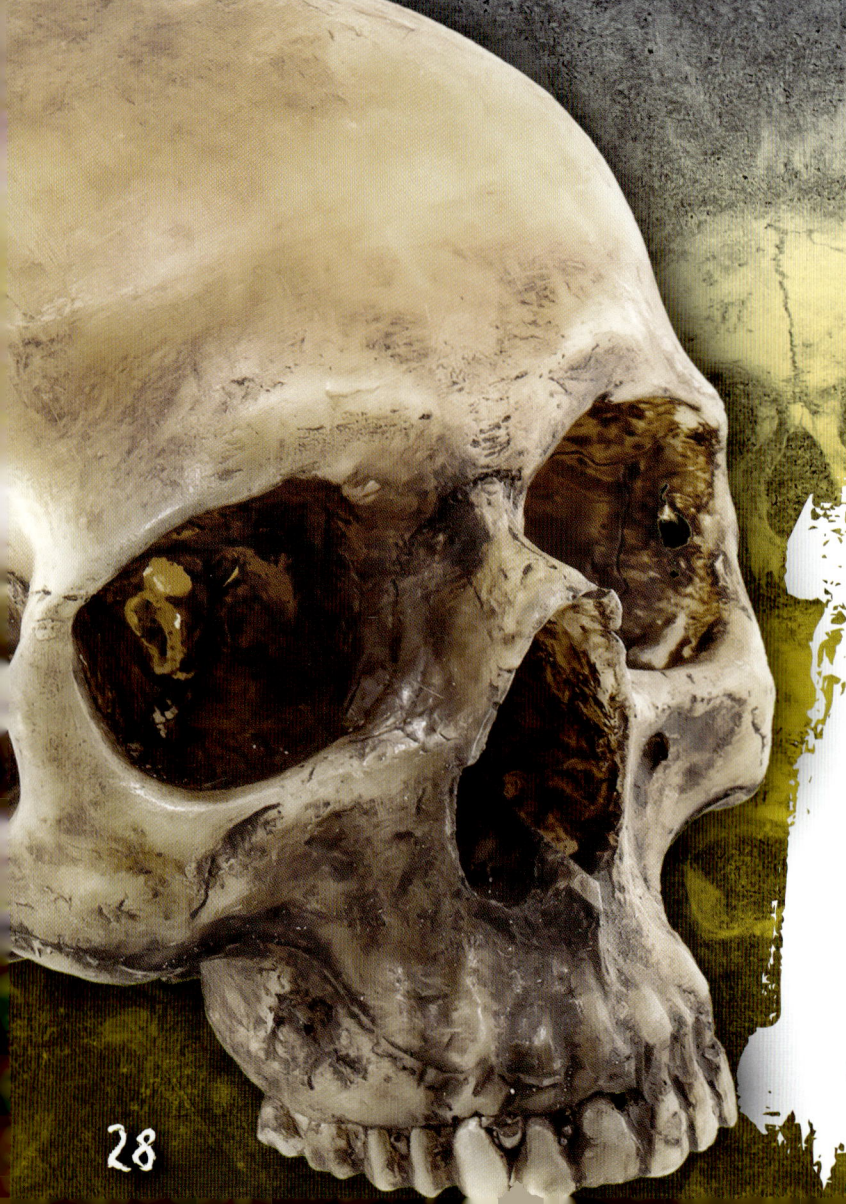

The walls of the tunnels are lined with millions and millions of skulls and bones – some are believed to be over 1,000 years old! If you're feeling brave, you can visit the catacombs and take a tour of some of the tunnels. But be warned: not all of the tunnels are open to visitors. These are walked by groups of illegal explorers, called cataphiles. Many of these cataphiles don't make it back out...

With the bones of so many people stacked underground, is it really any surprise that the catacombs are haunted? Many people have reported strange paranormal experiences from within the tunnels that can't be explained.

Don't Go Alone

In the early 1990s, a video camera was found along one of the closed, private tunnels. The camera had obviously been there for a long time because it was covered in dust and mold. People found a video on the camera that appeared to show a man exploring the catacombs alone. It shows him getting more and more lost within the tunnels, and more and more frightened. The final bit of **FOOTAGE** shows him drop his camera in fear and run down the tunnel into the darkness. No one knows what made the man so scared, and no one is sure if he ever made it out of the catacombs safely.

Debrief

Congratulations, investigator. You've made it to the end of this book and you've completed many investigations. Did you have any luck in tracking down ghosts? Don't worry if you didn't – there's still plenty of time and many more haunted houses to check. You could even check out some of the famous haunted hot spots that were in this book. Are you feeling brave enough?

Being a ghost investigator isn't easy, and many people fail along the way. If you think you're up to the challenge, take this book (and everything you've learned) with you to start your first mission as a ghost investigator. Some people believe in ghosts and some don't – but everyone has a good ghost story. However, it's your job to go out there yourself and investigate. Who knows, perhaps people will tell your story one day!

Glossary

advisers	people who give advice
apparitions	ghostly images
colony	a group of people who have settled in another country
communicate	to pass information between two or more people
convert	to change something from one form to another
denser	to be more tightly packed
fainthearted	those who lack courage
footage	a portion of movie or video film
fraud	to use lies or tricks to get something
frequency	the measurement of sound waves
host	to entertain guests
identify	to spot or recognize
interference	static that makes a radio or TV signal unclear and difficult to hear or see
mercy	kind treatment or behavior from someone who has power over someone else
naked eye	used to describe sight that is unaided by glasses, binoculars, or telescopes
network	a system of connected people or things
orbs	images of small circles on photographs, sometimes believed to be ghosts
Quakers	members of a Christian religious group founded in England in around 1650
sabotage	damage done to something in secret in order to stop something from going ahead or succeeding
skeptics	nonbelievers; people who question or doubt the beliefs that are accepted by other people
slaves	people who are owned by another person and have no freedom
society	a collection of people living together
solar flares	short, powerful explosions of energy from the surface of the sun
static	interference; having to do with electrical charges within an object
superstitious	believing that supernatural or spiritual forces control world events
surroundings	the things and conditions around a person or thing
suspicious	lacking trust
vocal	having to do with the voice

Index

B
bones 12, 28–29

C
cataphiles 28
cold spots 5, 9, 12–15, 17

D
death 4, 16–17, 23–24

E
energy 13
EVP 19–21, 23

F
fair 6, 8, 15
footsteps 18

G
Good, Sarah 23
graveyards 5, 28

H
Hampton Court Palace 16–17
Henry VIII 16–17
Howard, Catherine 16–17

I
interference 9, 18–21

K
knocking 18

M
Mumler, William H. 24

O
orbs 10, 12, 23, 25–27
Osbourne, Sarah 23

P
Paris Catacombs 28–29
Parris, Betty 23
photographs 5, 12, 24–27
precise 7–9
Puritans 22

Q
Quakers 22

R
recording 9, 19–21, 23

S
Salem 22–23
Seymour, Jane 16–17
spirits 4–5, 18, 23–26
static 19

T
temperature 9, 12, 14–15
Tituba 23

V
voices 18–20

W
Williams, Abigail 23
witches 22–23